AF326828

Some Mountains Removed

DANIEL BOUCHARD

SUBPRESS
2005

Printed in Michigan by McNaughton & Gunn
typeslowly designed

Cover photograph: *Fait*, by Sophie Ristelhueber, 1992
chromogenic print, 39 x 51 inches

Some poems in this collection were first published in the following
magazines, journals or anthologies: *100 Days: An Anthology*, *The Baffler*,
Bivouac, *canwehaveourballback*, *The Capilano Review*, *DC Poetry Anthology*,
eastvillage.com, *Mirage #4/Period(ical)*, *OASiA: Broadside Series No. 92(b)*,
The Poker, *Skanky Possum*, *Shampoo*, *Torch*, and *Vanitas*.

"Knives of the Poets" and "White Death This Exit" were published
as a Subpo Self-Pub chapbook titled *Two Poems* in 2001.
"Even Song for the Lost Pollinators" was published as a chapbook
by Phylum Press in 2004.
Some poems appeared in the chapbook *Sound Swarms and Other Poems*
published by Slack Buddha Press in 2004.

Subpress Books are distributed by Small Press Distribution
www.spdbooks.org

ISBN 1-930068-26-3
9 8 7 6 5 4 3 2 FIRST PRINTING IN 2005
SUBPRESS

Table of Contents

Leaves

Are bright?
Too dark
A night to tell.
In morning
Light I check
Notes to see
Silver reference
To Maggie's hands.

The hills
A laundry heap
Of color: xanthophyll,
Also anthocyanin.
The cold, less light they say,
Coerce truer
Colors on a stem.
All that deep green
Leaf juice leached
Into air? Depleted
Chlorophyll organs.
Sets of yellow sheets,
Flame on white tent poles.
Her fists
Bigger than quarters.

When hands were smaller,
Trees an activity, something
To tear pants on, cling to limb

Bark meeting skin
In lurch toward top.
What now but looking?
Orange hillside,
Carotenoid in oak,
Angled under sun,
Eat thru cold and
Sometimes sunny day.
Suddenly it's cocktail hour!
Sun acutely angled again.
Cocktail: a weird and wired word.
A word for parents, grandparents.
A word from our sponsors.
It's happy hour also, but
Haven't we been happy
all day?

Beanbag animals
Face down on floor.
The lamby has her
Jammies on. Jamie
Falls beside a
Ten ounce Dalmatian.

Cool air
Feeds fire's heart:
Purple, pumpkin, aster.
We walked seeking the cemetery
Covered in dead leaves,
Took a wrong turn
Twisted uphill a mile.

Cows chewing slowly watched us,
Slowly turning heads. Horses, too,
Bangs over eyes
Came toward the fence to meet us
Stopping to crop grass,
Forgetting all about it.

Jamie finished
Banana mush dinner
Brushed it thru his thin blonde hair
And took first step, 5:36
P.M., Mom
Stuffing stuffing into the bird,
Dad cutting squash into blocks.

I photograph Maggie by a window,
Her hands hold a bottle, hands big
As silver dollars. The marigolds
Are played out in the window box.
Faces frayed by weather, downcast
Under Orion.

I imagine it's warm in the city.
I imagine the single thin
Black road runs quickly
To a roiling black sea
From these fiery woods and farms
Under darkness.

Leaving the Northeast Kingdom

for Bill Corbett

You give excellent directions.
You were right: Peacham, South Peacham,
in fact, all of greater Peacham
is a splendid topographic coil:
pasture, tree, meadow,
green around white houses.
Thanks for the asparagus, the stories,
the drive about Montpelier, the chance
to see kingfisher and loon.

The hills rose soft and tough, like a baseball mitt
or a sack packed with bedfeathers,
they dropped off again steeply, the highway was empty
once off the backroads, no radio to speak of, a church
broadcast beckoned sheepish listeners "come back"
into the fold. Putting miles and clouds
behind me, pick-up trucks driven by kids,
the river ducked in and out of sight,
making way to Holyoke, Old Saybrook.
I crossed it a second time, after eating
at the *4 Aces*, for a quick route to 89,
speeding back into New Hampshire.

I see you at the kitchen table
dictionary open beside pepper shaker
and vase. Mockingbirds, hummingbirds,
interminable variations
of light and air.

Look

Tree
swallows

three
branches
in

family
nests
lodged.

Scream,
beak
and burst,

fly for the last
worm in ground.

Sparrow grass
          jump
by green
asparagus.

Folded
oak leaf

dropped,
a dead
          red
butterfly

motionless,
stopped

beside traffic
where it

fell
a sweet
fall day.

Crow
          atop
utility pole.

Swallows whirl
on surface
          snap
dragonflies up
coupling
in cool
afternoon.

Grievous, did we
denounce our
          ducks?
A neat
row arranged?

Or was it
in error

                our
grebe, unlike
a loon,
grown, gracious,
            and gone.

Either
            eye there
confuse osprey
with eider.
Neither.
Hi there.

Adore
            killdeer.
Four door.
Wheat beer.

Cormorant
            wind
imagine two
in the mix

between fray
of bridges
and yellow
            loosestrife.

The Actors House at Wellfleet

Sills and moldings
sag and split
in damp and mildew,
the sashes stiff,
frayed, the weights
sunk like ballast.

Its flourishing I imagine
like reading Edmund Wilson
nostalgia tapping
a florid tingling nerve.

Unsettled still, its workmen swept
away dust for folk who never wore shorts
even in hottest summer,
their sepia photos:
men and women we remember
as gentle and bright . . .
with the American friendliness and candor.

A sense of proportion: odd closets,
bookshelves built into walls. Things
taken in in an instant.

Look at the veranda logistics
or the broad baseboards
and floorboards equally broad:
it could not occur today

in a middleclass market.
The house is too small for the rich.

A squirrel slips between frieze seam and gable.

At the marsh edge a weeping willow
clear then of underbrush.
Ragged ropes dangle still
from high limbs, steel cars
once parked under it, gone
splendidly all to seed.

Flatirons found around the house.
Shrubbery overcomes the lawn.
Shingles crumble with the chimney.
The plumbing utterly fails.

One Week

Beach span, reach
around harbor to Long
Point and the light,
the sound to warn ships,
what ships? Foghorn
moans at random.
Let's not forget
we are here beside
the sea let's take notice
with ideas of what is in
the water, vague and cold,
to be tested like the week
itself. Mostly I want
to be here
on the folded white futon
where a dozen windows
admit ample light
and the sky is big
in all directions.
We have mockingbird
for neighbor, I wonder
what his rent is.

Below the swamp boardwalk
a bloated sea turtle, beached
in muck, claws fierce
      frozen
in atrophy and decay.

Thin yellow-striped snake
lifts its head above grass. Move
to make it move. Slither
for cover. Mosquitoes
will eat us in woods,
let's back
to the clearing, sit
on the shit-covered
picnic table, and watch
the Canada geese eat grass.

Dormant firehouse
on an active road.
Beside Engine Co. 5
a white-washed
shingle-weathered
shop of wide,
newspapered windows,
stairs absent from second floor
door. What's the story?
We'll take it! if we could,
take the driftwood lying about
like bones, collecting
in semblance some stems
of clay pipes, colored
glass smoothed in surf.
Mourning doves
retreat to eaves
as we walk by
and leave their young one
on the lawn.

The water ripples
like migrating eels.
A dog barks, happy
to be on vacation?
Bike paths wind thru
dunes amid scrub pine,
allow us somewhat to know
how the Pilgrims felt
first biking thru here
tho these giant bonsai trees
were bigger then
and more
Puritan too.

Sun blasted,
reading the Greeks
by the last fence post slouching
to sea. Greenheads buzz
about the ankles of Odysseus.

Driftwood Bits and Plastic Applicators

The center is grim,
a passive skull grin
among drums of bone.

Fish spines lie beside
dried grass, pebbles,
plastic, and sea-glass.

Shards of clamshell
make pumpkin teeth.
Cloud wisps mimic

bird wings in wind.
A beachgoer chases,
but only to breakwater,

a blue umbrella blown into surf.
Green and brown
bottle fragments

smashed and sanded.
Jagged pieces of jar
retain a bit of lip,

a thread, a letter or word.
Peach pits, peanut
and pistachio shells

among the hollow half-shells
of dead crustaceans.
Fiddler crabs face off.

Sanderlings romp.
Seaweed flaps in long
thin strips like shredded paper.

Jet exhaust visible
streaks past the three-quarter
moon. Shark sighting

and a school of blues.
The sun vanishes, a splash
of pink in the bay.

The Outer Lands are Ours

Did you find me a boring sponge?
Could you find me a boring sponge?
An eyed-finger sponge, mermaids gloves
or a crumb of bread sponge?

Buckets of starfish and hermit crabs fall
victims to the accumulative instincts
of children. Their parents pick catalogue lives,
worry and kick at images to carry
in sedately casual, expensive cars.

Crabs eat well: lugworm, blood
worm, clam worm and leech.
Why scuttle about what one should have been?
Arthropod or echinoderm.

Feldspar, iron, quartz,
shell bits and tiny shells.

A pirate tavern washed away
rounded stones rolling in nitrate
and sand, pottery bits, clay pipes and glass.

Take all the pictures you want.
Cigarettes: just throw these anywhere.

You have your choice of mollusks:
angel wing, mud snail, false
angel wing and fallen angel.

How the temperature dropped
when the ferry reached the bay.
In the bowl cod chowder,
shrouded sun, water threshold.

The islands contain
human remains.

Suburban Unnecessary Vehicle

When the corner store seems a hundred miles distance
around the bend in the road, the bend you never noticed
before, before the drastic scaling back of lilacs and forsythia
infused with a sweet chemical-coated mulch. This is the first sign.

The second sign is discovered on the white kitchen floor
where ice cubes of a billion years form and rise above
the window sills. Found in the excavation are a dozen dead
presidents with ancient and thin tongues like shoe leather.

When the vendor at Fenway sells his bags of Fuckin' A
then it's time to look for the next sign. Draw it from air
in a sale pattern of colorful apparel democratically arrayed
in a sponsored noonday sun. Their advertising typeface

praises the laugh track. All the oil stains on the pavement
are shaped like corporate logos. Even the green oil of the
hybrid corn poured forth in subsidies for a greener military.
The car wreck disturbs and delights the children: a sign.

When the elliptical rhythm is like a mill wheel dipping
deep, deep into the lazy gray water and spinning while
water falls from its carrying, or is poured, remember
that this is only a sign and that the days are upon us.

In the period of physical decline we may commission
a classical portrait. Yours forever ranks in the pantheon
of good taste and serves to charm even as it fails to inspire
care. This is the last sign before the final sign to come.

In myth the new is unclear, forever integrating, missing
abstract into substance, rash for the nuclear, veering off
again. All the music that roused you once will sell cars.
The stars never meant anything to you you could name.

Idle Music is the Devil's Band

This is how I learned to stop hating
the smug and arrogant, complicit folk
   inside the rampant
suburban ubiquitous vehicles.
This is how I taught myself
that my hatred of their crass
lifestyles of mobile and sanitized
sport and corporate offices burned
more energy than necessary

and my low-grade, high-minded hatred must stop
tho it conflict with or contradict the President's policy.
This is how I realized that, despite
the spacious righteousness in which I transported
   my endless and oblique hatred
in an easy-rollover luxury, my hatred
could easily and mistakenly crush
a less vitriolic man in an icy accident.
This is when I learned my hatred,
like war clouds that gather over a blue gulf,
   is bad for the environment.

And this is how I came to decide
to call Jesus on His cell phone.
Jesus works in Somerville
at the Somerville Theater
where He takes tickets today for the early show:
THE SUM OF ALL FEARS.   I thought He said

the Somerville Fears and I asked my Lord
who starred in the film. In the trailer,
as Jesus described it, a nuclear bomb
    "goes off"
and without giving too much away Jesus knew
the kernel of my question was an urgent fear
of nuclear war between Pakistan and India.

What side does Jesus come down on
when millions of Hindus and Moslems
are on the brink of mutual incineration?

This is how I came to know Jesus
is also
    politically disenfranchised.

Cat and Bird

A cat was out
as I was out
on an ordinary day.
A flock of starlings
hopped thru the lot
and the cat was up
to no good.
I was on my way out
but shortly came back
and saw a starling
stumbling out
from under a parked car
with broken wing,
his right, held out
like a small person
holding open
a sports coat on one side
(the way it angled out)
staggering on the asphalt
fearful eyes
betraying panic
taken totally by surprise
and his flock nowhere
to be found, certainly not
about the ground
where bright eyes glared
behind the hurt bird
in the dark recess
of a wheel well.

XXXI

I will always know this date
For the hanging of Nathan Hale
By the British, 1776, and also
The founding of the glorious
French Republic
In 1792. Today
Autumn is declared
Precisely at 1:27 P.M.
I will meet it for lunch
At Fort Washington, the oak
Leaves not even beginning
To turn orange, yellow, red and
Drop dead from branches
Above four heavy, black, useless
Cannons aimed
Recklessly at MIT, and the Hyatt
Regency by the river. Fifty-one
Years ago Russia dropped the bomb.
This is the birthday I share with
Tommy Lasorda, Martha Scott,
King Sunny Ade and Joan Jett.
I didn't get them a fucking thing.

Green apples
Abound in the grass
For me to pitch at barrel mouths.
One scores a lip and starlings
Chase it. Come here, birds,

Come here, I will read you "Birches."
Wind soughs gently and semis
Gear up
Toward lot exits.
The shadows long all day,
The day asleep in its musing.
I think I'll go out tonight
And spend some money,
Sleep in tomorrow, get up,
Throw a party. There are 100
Days left in the year.
Irving Berlin died 11 years ago
Today. He was only 101.

Some Mountains Removed

The Vietnamese grocers have all closed down.
Clapboard and brick
in soft snow light, and the ample light
of the big glass buildings.
Out of the subway tunnel, tracing
the slope of expressway, all the
three-decker tenements have flat tops,
and yards not enough to park a car.

Listen, the paraders have all gone home.
A cylinder packet in parapet bind. Pigeons
plug it as a delicate keep. Morning sunlight
soaks the snowbound square, the light
I remember when its absence evokes
petulant tenderness in ungrateful hearts
near the half-frozen river, a string
of traffic in rotor beads.

If property is theft, is theft of my property theft?
I don't mean the speculative dust flickering
in sunlight beams thru drawn shades, and not
the frantic filters set adrift while fishing
for stories of how others spent their lives
in pursuit of love, happiness,
self-congratulatory amazement
at the potato cell structure grammar's
recollection entices. And not the shades
they have become, nor the woolly blankets
drawn over you in the still-warm, still room.

In considering questions of reading
should one turn to books first for answers?
Enthrall to the means
of Blake's firm persuasion. Sights
parse motionless, turn a corner
where the walk turns from concrete
briefly to steel grille
above a subway vent big yellow
and orange machines lean
into lots for the tearing down. When
power erases the means to be free
you are free to burn the symbols of power.

What business was that machine
for? To rage against descent:
dissent to rant, not the comfort of
conglomerate, of images and villages,
a wrong wall to arm against matter
the mass builds and breaks under its
clumsy weight but never shall
totally shatter.

If this is New England February
can winter be far behind? The last
French Louis under lockdown longed
for a life of English first Charles. And guards
fetched it for him from the royal library,
and later his enemies got it for him
on the public scaffold. His triumph
contained in displays of regal wit,
his head severed in a laundry basket.

Springing our taut skin, warm to the ranks
of grasses lay down on a consequence of ants
extraordinary in their capacity to face
the highway, hear the hum, construe
a thrum of traffic to rush like a stream
in the westward hours setting
blankets crumpled under play, a sadder,
softer, slower tune, a lightness, lessening,
a lesson of allegiance in the car pack
departure, then amble and scuttle past.

The Old Town

Weird light: a dim beam ringed by dark
on the spotless concrete path. Subtle rumbling
in the sky, an underture for thunder, eerie,
while a little white girl skips to an idling car
where her mother yells from the driver's seat.

And the week-long heat wave is forgotten
after the first clean sheet of rain. I don't care
anymore what this place was, its thin line of traffic,
its vegetable cells of property, its stone walls
to keep it all neat, a quaint village history.

So long sprawling hamlet, we never were
true friends. How could we be friends?
The brownstone and brick "national historic"
structures. The underside of leaves show
when the wind blows them back. Blue

viscous clots of cloud sop over the trees,
move like a tide, quiet at intervals, and
then the wind roars, a flock of blackbirds fly
(together but to where?) and the day
darkens early. The library closes

"due to extreme heat," the magnificent oaks
blow in booming rustles wet when the rain
finally comes, not quick enough it seems,
tho the flash flood is judicious and gone soon
rinsing a trail of lichen-splattered fieldstones.

The highway columns support the overpass:
classic, original, American. Odysseus
never had it so good, nor do his bones rest
under the mown grass of the stately cemetery
in a manicured private lot: the final real estate.

New England Pasture (Prepares Research Seeding Facility)

Outside my workplace a building
is coming down. Humongous
yellow backhoes dance and pivot
on tank treads that shake the street,
scraping the concrete floor
and chipped tile from the ground.

This is a tough field for spring plowing.
Massive steel teeth comb and scoop,
push rubble into mounting piles.
Mangled, stringy rebar springs up
in a frenzy, freed from cement beds.

This little lot may resemble
remnants of Belgrade. A little army
of Guerette Corporation employs
machinery manufactured by Komatsu.

This is the celebrated lot
in recent photographs: its history lauded,
to commemorate "our" successes.
Radar and microwaves were born here.
Radar research began here
before the second world war,
in anticipation of same. Early airborne
microwave mapping (to be used
in search and bombing) took a picture

of Cape Cod and revealed
the true shape of the land.

How to find tanks cloaked under
the canopy of the mountain?
Meticulous destruction
ensures for the workers
safety from asbestos and toxins
in the fabric of the structure.

A headline pressed against the glass face
of the dispenser beside a hard-hat fence:
"We will bomb until we prevail"

The frame came slowly down.
Flatbeds cart away beams
stacked neatly for resale.
Light fixtures remain
on ceilings, dead wires droop
from floors of a sliced wing.

On the sidewalk is the season's first dead bee.

Movement

I have not read a book in days,
it's making me edgy.

      Ampersands
dropping from trees.

      Can't find
a damned thing. Down three flights
  up another three.

Why cart all these books around?
Dishes in newspaper. Murder
in newsprint dirties the hands.
I don't care
      for consumerism.
I would not kill for it.

Indonesian backlash
against seedling democracy: murder.

To go to work and find the same old stuff,
but the paycheck! Ah,
    it is too hot today.

'Muses' or recklessness? My fickle
attention, a will, not much else
      consideration

save love, and save
many other things.

Without diction
          contra or otherwise

where the immense
difficulty and also
          joy leap in?
(Note I do not
          say 'arise.')

Who is equity corp.?
Slicing your throat

with a profit
and a smile.

[1999]

Knives of the Poets

Juvenal, you're a shit, a misogynous prick
And this makes it very difficult to love you.
It's no time, and really, there never was
A good time, to be the underscored regurgitator
Of old republican virtues. Anyone
With a knack for debunkment knows
The undermining task of adjectival *so-called*.
Your virtues rot like peaches in a pile of offal.
Once when asked politely
Not to call women "sluts" you said
"Excuse me for not being politically correct"
And laughed, escaping the drubbing you deserved.
You are dead these many centuries but
Corruption's fecundity
Never sleeps. With precision I flick
Your indicatives like switches,
Disarm you adverbially;
Surreptitiousness, rhetoric, danger
Do not die when burned
In the phonemic fire of old virtues.

Your friend from Iowa
Bragged of his plastic connections
From his address book to his femur bone
Said he had gone down twice on a MacArthur genius
Or blew a Pulitzer winner, I forget which.
We don't care where the money comes from:
MacArthur, Ford, Guggenheim.

And since authorities are so openly
Hypocritical, face it: Mapplethorpe made many
Congressmen curious. They were forced
To kill the arts in order to save them,
Like any Communist town, desiring to make
The world safe for complacency. Even you,
Juvenal, you old fuck, know
This is far beyond their power.

There was never any danger
Only witches and little birds
On the swathe of steel blades,
Engines and sticks. So poetic
Vessels lie
Emptied of mendacity.
Not top of the line,
Just of the line. Unconventional
In a queerly conventional way. The poems
Never got under my skin like that,
They just whacked away at me
Like a meat tenderizer.
To not hear the feet pounding in the lines's
Periodic, irregular measure best improvised?
The poetry audience mutters a *hmph*
At recognized references.
Heraclitus or Whitman. *Hmph* says
"I read that" like the concert crowd who cheers
Hearing *whores on Seventh Avenue*—
"Hey, *I've* been on Seventh Avenue."

Today the kitchen possesses the peculiar

Smell of rotten wood
Drying in darkness, damp
Under curled linoleum, a Roman
Taste and the ripe,
Unauthorized vegetation
Swells outside the window, sweats
And sways in a breeze
Like an overweight person
In underwear stands before a fan turned to high.
An ellipse lawn of daisies and damask roses
Left alone from the mower on the chimney side.
And the president travels to Brazil or China
Issuing official apologies
For creeps, dictators, capitalists and thieves.
There are many people who sincerely believe
"America," personified, would fly
With Superman costume and cape.
(Beneath it a business suit.)
But the asshole who says "*America*
Must overcome its *Vietnam syndrome*"
Ought to be fed to the wolves.
So poets, spit specific invective,
While young, struggling for attention.
It may be your best hope to stave off poverty too,
A cultural 401k. Think heavily
In passives. Hear the dental tone
In rain patterns. Souls
Selecting their own.
Adversity dormant
For the moment.
These expressive variables turning on, beware

Asphyxiation.
When in doubt, palindrome.
When in despair, anagram. When I said
This will be fun I meant
This will be no fun
At all. If confused, collaborate.
If at a loss, dissociate. Never hesitate
Amid revision, stress emotive gestures
Not concision. No paucity, or lack of probity.
Cognate wise to reciprocity.
Give pause to gerrymandered clarity.
Solicit recidivists
For blurb austerity.
The old school may have been aggressive
But at least they had manners. Were they so
Delicate? Some called them gentlemen. Shut
The door. How a phrase might fixate
In mind for a moment,
An avid aphid sucks on enjoyable lush
But totally unemployable plant life.
The "not"/"but" as primary shaker.
The "as" as supine second fiddle.
The "or" a zinc mine of relative associates
And subject to charges of excessive subjectivity.
And good if read on a bus. Good
By ear.
I was happy when he mentioned his wife in a poem,
I stopped forgetting her name after that.
They think they invented poetry, the past
An indication of repression, patriarchy,
Racism, and the world as hateful as ever.

Now poetry seems to have vanished.
And that, they say, is part of the plan!
The labor force wear patterned
And pastel tablecloths. The workers fat
And not because they are paid well.
Fashioned loosely around the girth,
Language struggles, images and heat
In brainpan and heart.
Sloughing off dreck. Forced
Into a room of liars, sneeks, thieves,
Ayn Rand disciples, murderers,
Marketing managers, conmen
And capitalists.

No, sweetie, they are not joking. They are lying.
When they say "to make the world safe for democracy"
It should indicate something is wrong. Remember
So-called national security
Means the mace is aimed at you.
Flex your rights and become a traitor in their minds.
Some people take words seriously but
They are not always poets, be careful.
And then there are so few to speak with.
To be summoned, questioned, fed
A well-prepared (but not so well-delivered)
Statement and dismissed.
It was an odd union.
Suscept to be lulled.
You left the windows open and the shower on.
Rain filled June like a rinse cycle.
The shower in fact was not on.

The windows indeed were open all night.
In America they say, "it's not your problem."
It was kama sutra began in man
A suitable mantra for host marsupials
Plus the petal phase and pressure
Could not measure in American proverbs:
"Working together causes divisiveness."
Did I say America? I meant the States.
He is very very serious about poetry.
He has the social skills of a badger.
He is very tiresome.
I am sure he will win a major prize someday.

The imagination, its soothing uses,
At odds with boredom remains
Unredeemed: weekly complaints
Of paycheck drudgery
And what is worse, no sex to speak of
In the language, its practical applicability
For sensuousness
Other things similar to movies
And more. How language?
How the spoon reclines, the teacup cools
The nouns look awful
Arbitrary misnomers
And a public hazard at that.
Aphoristic rhythms ricochet
Off another's writing.
What is elite about lyricism?
Shall orgasms be democratic too?
The big sham of the radical

Transposed utopias
Into constructs of Art. Yes,
My egalitarian little lovely,
Keep licking right there. The
Torpidity of your tongue as it ignites
A singular patch of nerves
Is my right to remain silent
And the eloquence of trust between us.

Sunlight left to its own devices.
Gone from visible halves
Of atmosphere. I can't commit
My heart to where I thought once
It would be: always open, honest, free
From fears, not braced by
Slim, trivial regrets or
A fool's anxiety for the future.
I cannot correct in myself
Those fatal flaws I find well in others.
Because eyes choose and assemble
Quick imaginative meanings. As if intention
Were a better invention than kind acts
For transient strangers. Blue and black
Sky filling like fulsome liquid.
Citing Gramsci, poor man, as epigram
For hope: pessimism of the intellect,
Optimism of the will. Night turns
Obscene.

[1998, 2001]

On (An) Appointed Power

Always the rich kid. Arrogance like a weed
To get you really high. Always the dumb kid
Among the smarter rich kids. How to check
The power of the expensive hired hand?
A smart connection to get you out of a jam.
A statement or speech with fingers in the wind.
The virtues: self-promotion and damage control.

A veritable easy target
In the virtual free market
Of wit and sarcasm: you should be
Pitied like any puppet, one protected,
Picked and placed into power, surrounded
By power, lifted by the power of
An activist court: a made power.

I don't regret the dismissal of your
Predecessor. John Adams, retired,
Named his house *Peacefield* for the war
He averted at great political cost.
I don't lament your opponent's loss.
Where we trudged along to disaster
Now we shall sprint.

The White House fills with
A (com)passionate intensity.
But I won't worship bankers,
Jesus, or profits. Here,

An atlas shows the streets
Where the little children die
Whenever "America" cries.

[2001]

From the Word 'Go'

Rain in fervent mechanical gusts.
No more by midday but clumped
Humidity for wind less 15 degrees.
Thus autumn peeled bald by
Rigors of hurricane weather.
Hurrah, whether a capella,
Authoritative but unacclaimed
Imperious delay. Audio distortion
Crowd defect, hissing sibilant
Animal sounds. Its liquid state
Lies in, wracked up, writhing—
Is it wrong to have written that?

A chronicle comes to its close
On tombstones and grass tufts. Ream,
Yard, lint and postal
Code zip disk begin again
Today on bare boughs in bright
Yellow, bright orange, bright
Red spatter onto black streets.
Hard to come by conduit clarity,
Something which no one will agree
To but all can enjoy in the
Calvinistic sense liberty of
Conscience hath brought free
Verse but no free parking
At Roger Williams park murder
And magnolias, the night so well

Lit and convenience stores so
Convenient to see stubs suck
In the gutter for governor's
Revenue so much false silver is
Down (as it were) the drain, rubbed
By edges of tessellated coin.

The Apartment

I wake up in the surface of a Frank O'Hara
poem. A weeknight, I've been watching
the late show: that old film of Billy Wilder's
—*The Apartment*—and from the movie I dream of living
in post-war New York City
        where everybody dresses

like the all-white cast of *The Apartment*
and the prosperous, bracketed, dull 1950s
suddenly grow wilder than what we're told
because everybody seems anxious to sleep
        with anyone but their spouse,

and the show is so campy but it's not gay
which I feel is an insult to Frank O'Hara
who, like Jack Lemmon, went to college
in Massachusetts. I dream of living
when those midtown steel erector sets
        like upright metal ice-cube trays

rose above handsome but dilapidated rows
of stone apartments, scrapped as slums
for things like Lincoln Center, and everyone
seemed eager to cheat on their spouse
        and dressed very decently.

No, of course I never knew Frank O'Hara,
but am among those who meet to talk about him:

don't you think the young Jack Lemmon looked
a little bit like Frank O'Hara? Maybe that's not
true, but I wonder if poetry will outlive celluloid
in this renaissance atomic age.

Opening Calyces

Who was it I dreamed of last night
I may have known outside of
these piss-relief dreams of romance

suddenly she was with someone else
I knew him then she was someone else,
an open window screened from the flights

of curious intruders I woke under a light
wind, rain, all of a stifled season pouring
into the room, jet engines slicing a saturate

sky, small, plated vibrations, like a motor
on my back. Lately, I refuse dreams
on the brink of waking: a pang of

dread, some duty, an errand to be made.
Imprecise, I recognize direction,
unconscious, a festoon carton of tea,

hexagon cells of wax plates welded
to walls of dripping honey. Concise,
like a cartoon, I stood barefoot

on a dirt path, something stuck
in the crease or hinge
of my toe: an ant, its head embedded

in skin ridges I can't shake him but
flick carefully and once free roams
in circles, repetitive and small,

to regain bearings, and wander back
to the pearl-colored sacs strewn inside
the rolled rhododendron leaf,

where nurses clamor in mulch, below
involuntary dreams of bee lines,
Blaschka's glass flowers, a stone

bridge with paint-shot towers
and full faces of leviathan
or dolphin approached from the water,

a porous approach to sleep, a portal.
Dreaming, not of nature, not
the impulse to move, not reading;

my eyes move over pages
of blurred lines, and opaque,
invented narrative. I wake

on sheets of big yellow flowers
and the book is open, dropped
on my chest, ears drumming,

as bees in honey drum I dream
of my own body weight, indistinct
and separable from the beating heart.

A Gallery Pass

after the photographs of Sophie Ristelhueber

An overturned tank
beside its severed turret
is a camera cartridge
aimed north or south.
The whirr of advance
is heard as it happens:
explosions in the folds
of distant hills. In the shutter,
effacement or incision.
One doesn't see
as it happens, this
invasive surgery. (Err
to surface.) Trenches
and entrances
to underground bunkers.
Bury, efficiently, the enemy
where they stand.

An artist "stands
like an archeologist."
Square serial shots
hung from craft
in the liberated desert
out of allied hangars.
Spent ordnance, burnt
and shot, blasted cars,
rusted trucks and

buses along a treeburnt road.
Not documentary, not
witness, not this thick
zipper up to the neck
(antiseptic post-op)   yet
the woman stands like Venus,
her naked back to the lens.

Brass shells half-buried
in yellow sand. Here
comes the artist
to confront "reality."
To shoot the ruins.
Forgotten veneer
of the unlucky. Souvenir
dust, bent metal frames
made unlucky by fire,
and charred scrapbooks
place earth's millennial
kin, a pocked
moony surface
asking does the skin
of the pachyderm
tear like canvas?
Red cross-hatches
where skin rips.

A delicate anesthetic
of violence: good and
bad (mostly bad). Local
aesthetics: look at

the prints, horror at
the evidence but no trace
of the tread's path, no frame
for the cut's end
tho the stitched flesh
is clean you wonder
that the body healed at all.

Fenestra Vestibuli

I.

  In a fight
for the crumb two birds twist,
  tumble and flap fumbling
    on cement.

Two fists of feathers one pinned
   flips off
     his adversary.

The most violent encounter ever seen
   between birds
        till one
breaks in flight for the treeline
   south of the fight scene,
   the opponent pursuing,
      still going.

Magnetic minerals
  of the steep bank
draw eyes above the swift water:
and a thrush with a heavy touch of brown
   on the upper wings, and white
  rings frame the dark eyes.

  A haughty grackle on the picnic table
rubs his bill

against green-painted boards,
  retches, bloats like a burp,
all ruffled up, and shrieks.
            (He is preparing for a date.)
  A purple sheen, oil in a puddle — black
  from afar — beak
  open   yellow
  menacing eyes.

White-bellied swallows
dart out from under the eaves
of flat-bottomed boats.
  Broods squawk in the rafters
above the patio gift shop.

2.

Relief in hard rain,
      a wash of the humid or
for the brain an easy rain.

I hum the thunder. Perched
up on the porch like a bachelor
or blackbird, the flood
prophecy of weatherheads
has in evening come to pass:
no moon, no stars
but the headlights of minivans,
the oscillating swish, swish
of a lone cyclist headed home.

3.

The yellow
warbler

hovers above
an orange flower.

Grass blades can
snap like boards,

a pop can
collapse, a car

wreck, glass
shatter

and sound
flies in the

delicate ear bones
of confusing warblers

their more
certain Latin

nomenclature,
a Saturday

beak probe
for bugs on

the great day-
lily towering

over yewlings.
Split echo,

soft tissue
lead verbs thru

tiny chambers:
sirens reel

inside, foot-
steps on brick,

jet wake,
incessant

tread
of red ants.

Sound Swarms

Tired enough to sleep in
      someone else's bedroom
against the double-groove
      of mattress, behind a curtained,
glass-panel door. People
      chatter and laugh in the next room.
The sounds swarm
      in small canals.

It's not a conundrum after all.
      Blake, after all,
believed the world flat.
      No pall nor clouds hang
over those who will not live long.

The wind chill is like
      needles in the face.
We live among men who won't mind
      incinerating half the earth
for the idea they were right. Among
      the gone half
anyone who ever said it won't matter
      when you're gone
will finally be right.

Traveling is the pleasure of rising
      mornings to watch other folks
go to work. To have met them

for an hour, when handling
their books, think of them, small
        images to care and carry
as long as you can retain them.

William Blake appeared to me in a vision.
He spoke to me. He said,
        "get your damn feet off the sofa."

Confusing ears disable. Double.
        Variable. Warble. One book
made him a believer and
        another talked him out of it.

The Fancy Memory

The presidents Lincoln and Roosevelt dined with me at the reception, and I asked them if the sanction of the State was necessary to complete or complement the combination of sexual, emotional, spiritual, intellectual and financial unions.

Lincoln answered, "the state is an arbiter and also an administrator. It can be judicious if it is powerful. It can be tyrannical." He cut his meat with slow and long strokes of the knife.

Then I asked: "can justice exist without power?"

He replied: "some believe it can; those who make stances against an oppressor are not merely waiting for their own opportunity to oppress."

The dinner was served family style. An efficient man, assistant to Roosevelt, carved a roast chicken at the sideboard. A crisp shallot dropped to the floor while he worked.

Roosevelt began to speak but his predecessor interrupted him: "All wedding days," he said, "all marriages, have a beginning, middle and end."

Roosevelt fixed a cigarette into its holder.

Lincoln spoke: "A year has passed with good health and an abundant harvest. We have no enemies in foreign lands."

I heard this with some wonder.

After dinner Roosevelt nodded to his man and was wheeled to the patio for a smoke. Lincoln and I drank coffee and watched the bride and groom dance slowly on the wood floor. An ice sculpture of Venus stood on a table in the hall; water dripped quickly onto the peel-and-eat shrimp from the tips of her melting fingers.

Lincoln spoke of Emma Goldman, someone he admired, and her desire not to be the forger of her own chains of slavery. Lincoln wondered aloud why Americans choose to have so few children.

I asked Lincoln how he felt about being called "Captain."

Sleeping with Muses

Asleep in the cozy corners
recently swept of humble dust,
under the single painting by a major
Flemish artist. Dozing on the bench
that reads yes you may sit here. You must
pay admission and the mission portends
of great black Puritan portraits,
no lack of grandeur here. Let's sleep
in the museum of enormous windows.
We are not at a loss for curious antiques
and the patina is rich brown, rich
in vernacular like the bold black
lines (some call it form) on the canvas
I heard the schoolgirls call big ass.
Let's go sleeping in the film room
with the new-smelling all-surface
carpet. The lens is a life here, our life,
and it lends credence to dreams
with rapid focus, abrupt transitions,
strangely plausible events, keen for detail
of the otherwise (unfilmed) mundane.
A montage of the conscious to stir there
a larger collage of sleep. We won't even take
off our shoes. Life is not taking off
shoes, it shows how to frame grandly
and call it by name. Our heads
droop and dip forward as we go
under; pray, eat, travel, and work hard
in our dreams. There will be a train,

an allegory, a woman with a lovely
figure, smartly dressed. We sleep fast
and cold in these stone and plaster rooms.
Up in the rotunda a bat beats its wings.
Nodding off. There was a blue vase
of burnished flowers. There were hats,
teacups, and impressive educations;
and in the foreground red velour, black
cats, and strident flags of the most
aggressive nations. And I saw women and men
sorted by class and dress and occupation.
And I thought I knew what it meant
to take vacation. But is this
Art, sister, you who know my perturbation?

The Painting School of Fibrillating Landscapes

Who wastes his life, in the mix and fray,
not in terms of pay, today the final score:
        the poet or
                the sports anchor?
  The one pursues
excruciating
  minutiae

        but never let them say
"he meant well" or other such
insults. They won't ever locate my heart
        "in the right place."

Today the Allies pounded the Axles
in a stunning victory not at all
  surprising. The game left thousands
of homes destroyed, thousands of
fans missing, maimed or dead.

Much of the falling flakes
      sink into wet paint,
the white already on its way
to being not quite that usual absence
  as the visual facilitator
saw it under the shade
      of braced steel supports.

The emissions are
immeasurable:

absorb on surface what probably was
dull blue or green
   or a little of both.

A noxious art, relieving lung capacity
and the otherwise unwanted wastes
of the unwarranted scene, a flash seen,
motion overhead, driving
toward or away, it is the way
to other places, to lie beyond
   the boundary:
            focus and frame
tiny defibrillations
   tumble
     the rough
textures,
         reverberations
   and rations
   of unexplained
   ravines.

   Drip and drip
from granite ledges.
This is the whole
flippant universe.
I see a fractal,
terribly distorted.
Did some lens get this
office poached? Donald
Rumsfeld of the girded loin.

You presume: you
presume anarchy I
presume. Forces
for equality, anti-coercion.
   Their enemy rides
            in formation
on horseback, motorbikes, tanks;
take weapons and orders from interests
of those who have interests in banks.

Poetry goes at the war but poetry
is a provincial city. It's a city of glass
   and social conditions.
      It's the ruins we inhabit,
and the outlook is violence, a forerunner
of philosophical thinking, political thinking

"for instance"
Xtianity will never inspire
   great artists
         to its service again.
Thusly Pop thrives
   on the carcass
         dumbly ignoring
            a trembling phoenix.

In "The Ruins of Springfield Walmart"
            "for instance"
shepherds in tattered Nike gear wait
   and warm to fire on the filthy sales floor.
               Smoke rises,
wisps and firs past an absent ceiling.
      "Oil on Beach,"

oil on canvas:
   a bearded leader and a robed throng,
        poised by tumultuous waters:

"Harry Truman Destroying Pharaoh's Army"
   evokes,   "for instance"
        the heroic
   the instant before sea waves
crash and disperse them in surf.

I see what I see; the eyes have it.
Birds are watching me. They are watching birds.
        Conspicuous: a jam
of limbs and lines blurred
behind the collective colors

black, small-bodied
   on a green field, a purple pavement,
   a stone ledge
below the steel bridge
   holds plastic caps of every kind and color.

        Dead long enough
   overnight snow floats
        on the downy nape,
wings bobbing gently
   in the ebbing water,
   some splayed red and pink
giftwrap ribbons tangled at the throat

        Hades faces
environmental crises.

Christmas is Balmy

The starfish chases the sea-snail
in the digression of the lobsterman's
story: the sea-snail runs for its life.

"Oh Time, Strength, Cash and Patience!"
            as it goes in *Moby Dick*;

Stones sand the
            busted glass

                  on harbor shores,

mingling with plastics
            and tons

                  of broken red brick.

The eider ducklings and their mothers are brown.
They stay close to the rock when an eagle's around.

The seagulls rise furiously

      when the eagle strikes the island

            like a missile.

Christmas is Bombing

Melville tells us there is nothing
more insignificant
than having a book of poems published.

Skimming with easy vituperation,
the reading seethes. Sees?
"He had a dream and it shot him."

From where beyond the inky afterburn
do the scholars and scripters come? Disaffected
by profit, a thesis scrawled with a cube
of sharpened blue chalk:
"Walt Disney in Cryogenic Hell"
measures against the hulk of the waterlogged *Walter Scott*
that Twain saw as a cause of war, the *casus belli,*
belies the volunteering of Huckleberry Finn,
dead at Antietam; his boyhood friend
lived to see Buster Keaton in
The General.

I bet the president knew how to get seriously
fucked up; I bet he knew how to do some
serious damage.

The national tele-drama will have us believe
a series of intelligent, honorable people
making honest mistakes in democratic endeavors.

Forcing myself back
over lengthy paragraphs I spaced on
                while imagining my own death out
of those sentences, with comedy in kind
                but lacking the chivalrous notions
"the house full of men, yonder, with guns!"

                But where is the genuine humor toward the war?
    If the slogans of abolishment are gone
like horses and wagons from these streets
                or the stagnant vocabulary of an obsolete trade

what seer dulls our grief with delicious irony
                and raises mirth first when the missiles whistle?

Even Song for the Lost Pollinators

Pumpkin scars of the living-room décor lapse. **Then how should I begin . . . And how should I begin? (T.S. Eliot, "Prufrock")** Who has the power to inflict real pain? Fog stuck in orange and yellow trees across the river. Who has the considerable power to hurt? **My way is to begin with the beginning. (Byron, *Don Juan*, Canto 1)** A split or gap in leading turns the avenue into a venue. "Pun, fact, banality" (Zukofsky, explaining line 12.) The sun is done, scrunched under the grim sink of tree lines, grinding the red western hills. Lights race again at a distance in fine lines to untoward towns. **Beginning, then, with the beginning, in a purely inductive way . . . (Peter Kropotkin, *Memoirs of a Revolutionist*)** Arguments collapse, air sucked above dust. (This is not what I wanted.) Look in the past: not an answer to your question, here is, Keston, the best line I find: *profiles of hope glisten eyes.* Despair as compassion, remorse for horror but, as in Defoe, these things subside and our regular lives go on with a function it seems like carelessness until the moment we are faced with our own deaths the moment we face again. **He sat down, opened the book, and with his elbows firmly planted on the table, and his hands to his temples, began at the beginning. (Thomas Hardy, *Jude the Obscure*)** Hard paved sugar roads, the ones in the back, easy to split like a shingle and spit. **Begin anywhere. (Rachel Blau DuPlessis, "Draft 26")** We met late in the week in summer. A religious cult recruited me into a pick-up game of volleyball on the New England green where seven years before a man became the only Gulf War dissident to set fire to his gas-soaked skin. She taught political theater and improv to activists attending a week-long seminar on radical economics. No roses: pitchers at a brewery, bee-filled bushes and poison ivy in the cemetery before Emily Dickinson's grave. **And so, together, as one, we shall begin. (William Carlos Williams,** *Spring and All*) Squash. Gala apples, tomatoes, basil this late. And cukes, three for a dollar. A dripped out or dropped in a shift: we all—well I—we all saw a well or wall. These bones are serious inroads; intent cracks teeth in rows. **Poetry begins with tendentiousness. . . . Work begins long before one receives and becomes aware of the social command . . . Preliminary work goes on continuously. (Maya-kovsky, "How to Make Verse")** The second Patricia's brash rasp from scalp to scab, paralyzing, trapezing, grappling a feign stake drank with indelicacy: "this is precious time; I have to write." **Our world today is only in the beginning of knowledge. (H.G. Wells,** *The Outline of History*) The guileless trout, the honest duck. They savored the blade in the marketplace for ketchup where xenopho-bia is measured by anti-bureaucrats against a mark of what cops tolerate in the customs of immigrant populations. **History is a tangled skein that one may take up at any point, and break when one has unraveled enough; but complexity precedes evolution. The** *Pterapsis* **grins horribly from the closed entrance. One may not begin at the beginning, and one has but the loosest relative truths to follow up. (Henry Adams,** *The Education of Henry Adams*) Faulty mechanism switch; five locomotives & nine cars containing plastic pellets, bricks, railroad ties, flour animal feed, and ammonia spilled off the tracks Tuesday morning also containing lumber, newsprint, animal bones to make gelatin, hydraulic cement, miscellaneous chemicals, corn, some cars empty except for some detergent. The engineer and the conductor got safely off the train traveling to Portland, Maine from East Deerfield, Mass. (27 MPH in 30 zone) near Route 2 and Princeton Road, fire officials said "There were no occupied houses near the site of the accident." **Begin at the beginning, / find the end. / Remember everything, // forget it. Go on. (Robert Creeley, "Things to Do in Tokyo")** The interstate north is like a church aisle; our eyes gaze up to heaven or the horizon. Rackstraw Downes: "The indistinguishable tangle of razor-wire and branches." In dusk light tree lines are dark like the shadows of hills, so unlike the avenues of hulking sidelined buildings. **I see through your weapon / the earth is a star / let's begin at the beginning. (Andrew Levy, "South of Intention")** All the tiny possibilities present in the belly a zygote the size of rice grain, the book said a month and the tube to become a heart is pulsing already. Bulging coned paper of a wasp's nest on the ultrasound screen. **Everything was to be begun; not only that, but unlearned, and then at last begun. (Muriel Rukeyser, *The Life of Poetry*)** In the apartment life continues with oven timer buzz and rush of running water. Otherwise we are warmed, warned of death and likely privations of a less entrenched oligarchy. Where did she go? I lay where she was, the cushions still warm. **. . . therefore to write no matter what begin again . . . (Bernadette Mayer, "I Want to Talk About Reason, Riddle")** Shakespeare makes her heart skip a beat. Shakespeare makes her hurt skip. A thump like gardening, a bounding rubber ball, quick squeaks of sneaker, a stagecoach robbery, a garden of mind's delight. **The poem / is complex and the place made / in our lives / for the poem. / Silence can be complex too, / but you do not get far / with silence. / Begin again. (William Carlos Williams, "Asphodel, That Greeny Flower")** Now the cold is here, how that coal is heat or should I reviser with my sight again? Cats or some kind of animal visibly jumping spines:

an aging Borges, the serif type of another time decries the letters of a poet, an historian. **Never hesitate to go back to the beginning. (Alice Notley, "The Prophet")** Imagine a bio >   being written of John Wieners: where he was in what >   particular order, who >   he did or was done by, and a Faith Hill – Exclusive >   Performances, Videos, & more faith.yahoo.com. **And yet—one must begin somewhere. (William Carlos Williams, *The Great American Novel*)** Turn the intensity of staring vocables ready to fuck with you, a fight for prosody you won't wear a hat inside here again, getting ready and revved up: slabs the size of Cleveland are dropping everyday. Ground like pepper over the stove. Around supper attractively packaged retail toxins come one, rebarbative, come all ye fateful. **You can read a book over and over again until you remember everything and even then you can read it over again if you begin at the beginning. That is very important about reading a book over again you must really begin at the beginning . . . When I began writing I was always writing about beginning again and again. In *The Making of Americans* I was making a continuous present a continuous beginning again and again, the way they do in making automobiles or anything, each one has to be begun, but now everything having been begun nothing had to be begun again. (Gertrude Stein, *Everybody's Autobiography*)** Pigeons and backhoes, men in white shirts, neckties blowing in breeze, and the sound of vehicles moving east. Alive in that water, hard to believe. I think I know what a fish is. What is belief? **To begin again / is no gain. (Ted Pearson, "Refractions")** Minnows visible, fish shadows flash over the floor of paint-fading metal. Then a carp of some kind shadows the bottom junk and mud. Two feet long, feeding in shallows, and two more appear. Suddenly a helicopter passes and the big fish vanish. **My brother began at the beginning with definitions. (Bertrand Russell, *Portraits from Memory*)** What did you see lifting the lid of the box that is usually closed? The powerful did not wish to be seen. The unattractive was often withheld. When the thick lining, resplendently sewn, tears it is called a rent. Some people imagine there's a past extant (in arrears) and its glory is always gone. **Begin again. (William Carlos Williams, *A Novelette*)** All this and the cat's tail tied with pink ribbon, wrapped in a gift box. The cat watched the neighbor unwrap it from beside the post. **Start again. (Philip Whalen, "Treading More Water")** Savage breakfasts, the under of getting home by sunrise tho it's more likely the lights of sidewalk cafés and drug stores burn brighter than the effluvient of saying yes to the all-powerful invader. **I am interested in those who begin at the beginning. (Nathanial Tarn, "The Great Odor of Summer")** Before the flagrancies there is no guess to reaction, who folds first under hope, the first infliction, or blossoms leaving behind the work or the refuge of religion and education and the black magic of the arts. **What am I to do? / One must begin somewhere. / Begin what? / The only thing in the world worth beginning: / The End of the world of course. (Aimé Cesairé, "Notebook of a Return to the Native Land")** Fire of old sticks, branches, and boards flipped into fire and ants who live here. There's a pall and it's over. And over redaction a pall-bearer bears standards and walks straight. **Begin again. / It is like Homer's / catalogue of ships: // it fills up the time. (William Carlos Williams, "Asphodel, That Greeny Flower")** Exit to Boston Common to street: J Quincy Adams's home which stood on this site … **after a minute Humpty Dumpty began again (Lewis Carroll, *Through the Looking Glass*)** son CFA born 1837 minister to Great Britain during the

Civil War; a tablet placed 1925 Boylston and Tremont, Common-
wealth of Mass. RMV, a donut shop beside a liquor store Chinatown
Orange Line stop Sons of Liberty Tree. "Allright Parking." *Happy
24th birthday Laura / Bye Henry* Ironworker graffiti Washington
and Boylston broad horizontal framework of new hotel freezing
day before Thanksgiving *Jill K is a babe / Bye Mary Ann* the Essex
Deli and Grille where the folks and I **You begin again all over
more or less . . . (Samuel Beckett, *How It Is*)** breakfast Friday
mornings the Essex Street stop closed ruins of a kiosk where Doug-
las hung by his hands for a photo after the cemetery stop on the
Common I lay down with Quakers—Friends—some summers back
tall yellow grass head rest beside the slate Paramount Pictures façade
stripped to brick preserve the marquis staircases bared *Publix The-
atres* handsome building next is federal. Name? Fifteen arcades dirty
white rococo Keith Theater, The Opera House, old Adams restau-
rant now "Yesterday's" and an alley, continuity break, the Modern
Theatre top boarded windows. **Nothing so difficult as a beginning
/ In poesy, unless perhaps the end. (Byron, *Don Juan*, Canto 4)**
A circle of bared breasts rings Brewer's fountain and the fountain
in Philadelphia on the Parkway near the Museum. Running water,
Pan's pipes of a dust pan in a cracked cement pool. **How to begin?
/ And now I have. (James Schuyler, "The Morning of the Poem")**
Flashes in night's storm pass with a push or pressing against my
windows the lightning introduced by thunder and a wave of rain
applauds. It's all hoard and display, all hoard and show. The perfumed
commuters are a patient lot, and they've all worked patiently for
what they've got. **For the present I do nothing but read and write
in our room, read and write in the libraries. It is a little annoying
for you, I admit; it is not all what I had led you to expect; but in**

everything one must always begin at the beginning. (Pierre-Joseph Proudhon, letter to his parents, 1832) Here in the States the Friday after Thanksgiving is a holiday, except for firemen, cops, hospital staff, fast food workers, and me. I boarded the train at 10:10 P.M. and eavesdropped on my fellow pilgrims. A black man talked about his apprenticeship as a steelworker in Boston. He liked it. A group of married white men and women sat across the aisle drunk and toothless. "I'm going to strip down and hit the bed. Going to sleep all morning. Going to sleep all morning not get up till 9 or 10." **These things that you call Finish'd are not Even Begun; how can they then be Finish'd? The Man who does not know The Beginning never can know the End of Art. (William Blake, *Letters of William Blake*)** Whitman's fury is pent whereas Whittier whose "outcropping love of heroism and war, for all his Quakerdom, his verses at times like the measur'd step of Cromwell's old veterans" while a California town from which came a would be capable Cromwell who fitfully fought Commies even where they were not **Pause. / And begin again. (Kenneth Patchen, "What is the Beautiful?")** Orwell scripts the pilot for a mythos-heavy tele-drama of ironic realism. (This is not what I wanted.) Bare iambic feet. The song plies mood. **. . . it must begin again. (Rachel Blau DuPlessis, "Draft 19: Working Conditions")** There's the channel I drove under, a tunnel to the other mass and lakes pocked on land, half-frozen, half warming. The poet lives in folios, notebooks, or code to upload to mind and harp monitors of race. **I can begin again so often that I can begin again. (Gertrude Stein, *The Geographical History of America*)** Planes rumble, ascending six miles or so east from Boston headed south over the towers of the city beside the guttural sucking of the coffee maker. A white pipe. A narrow chimney. An insurance office building. **. . . I see I must begin / Right at the start . . . (W.H. Auden, "Letter to Lord Byron")** Now the hawks are gone from their regular riverside nesting, a group of five in new construction, big as chickens ambling over the road. **V. You must begin at the beginning. // P. The beginning! But where is the beginning? (Edgar Allan Poe, *Mesmeric Revelation*)** In the crash of columns new rivers are born, new flow. Coffee and ready the enter: read a letter, or notes for more poems. **To begin with to begin over, to do it again . . . (Bernadette Mayer, "Agoraphobia")** Trick types on the page read subversion like you hear a president's voice promise painless death and money as you are killed for your own good, tho the minority hatches quietly a conspiracy on the tab of a god robbed of an 'o'. Disbelief belies from 'f' to 'd', well damn your eyes in effigy. **I then thought to begin. (Jennifer Moxley, "Stem of the Tree of Orestes")** For the lost pollinators and breed of final amphibians beginning finals whistle thru interactive spheres resigned to raining missiles and fear divides like cells, compassion issued for victims and decrees sprung forth to give shape and everyone asked to go shopping. **Greek and Latin are very well, but I sometimes feel we ought to begin at the beginning. (E.M. Forster, "Other Kingdom")** The one-liners of pet owners. Well damn your eyes. **. . . this love song which always / begins again? (Robin Blaser, "Delfica")** In the poet's death we are impoverished in the loss of their work, thru its absence, neglect or erasure. By their death we only learn more from them. **After a night's solitude they were always ready to begin again. (Virginia Woolf, *The Voyage Out*)** In photographs, or rotographs, Copley Square is bisected by a road that began as a railroad bed when the Back Bay was actually water and this road takes you to barn country and the Berkshires; the

WPA Guide documents the route. **Pressed to begin again / return to morning / sun & its pursuit . . . (Dale Smith, *The Flood and the Garden*)** Did he just say "exposing himself to God?" and should I capitalize "God" as I'm guessing he did? As I capitalize divine on guffaws in lowercase just in case. **Unable to begin / At the beginning, the fortunate / Find everything already here . . . (George Oppen, "A Language of New York")** And they sought how a beehive is liable to behave when provoked, that is, stoked like live fire.

The Rest

I have the rest
of my life to be

sorry I do not
do this, do the

other. When I
think of how

time is spent,
think getting,

spending, getting
and in delirious

details the devil's
ministers deliver

time and time
again I have

the rest
of my life

for thank-you
and all

the notes and
I know it.

The Winter Range

Here is the black stuff, steaming and hot,
pumped in morning to get going. Not oil:
these grounds are more easily tossed, all
compost on another lot and later at the gas
pump a rush from the nose starts up again.
The first jets rise sharply a few miles east.
They rumble overhead and pass.

Finish with lists and count syllables.
I have not yet begun to write this
provisional situation. I walked yesterday
between financial Boston and Chinatown:
the old curbs crushed down by trucks,
new asphalt fills the street like black snow.
The low stone buildings just provide,
two absent across a lot and scars
remain on walls of squat
neighbors. It rained so much, and look!
a drowned rat flat on his stiff back,
small teeth poke out. To walk past
lots of busted blue and green glass.
A day of clementines and coffee,
the winter afternoons, pull down
der sturm und drang, I say
pull down the dang storm windows.

Pull back to a map
from the 18th century. Found in
the ground, those thin-lipped margins,

traces of an ink shore, a briar swamp where the Y
now stands. In rhetoric fang
the kerning elicits: be kind toothers
in small caps. Tongue
beside bitewing to hold. See a history
of title pages, progress in the printing
industry. Where the authorities drug
the insane to face a saner
execution, this is not utopia. Utopia
is not paradise. It discusses the shock
and awe of music. Utopia is a place
where someone is not trying to kill
you, where you do not pay for
someone else's sins. How things
get broken and left
in sharp heaps, shards, little piles
never meant to be here, it happens
like the lozenge yellow tomatoes
in beaded dirt below a firm, fat-headed
sunflower leaned over a high picket
fence. We struggled and dug
the roots of the juniper
in the sandy soil a sleeping beetle
hind leg up in winter's sleep, we
didn't want to wake it.
I have the poet's dual instinct to say
on the one hand it doesn't matter and
the other to set everyone straight.
I must have more hands than that.
It's cold in this rain, my hands will burn
with blood inside when I get home

to the dutch oven steaming above thyme
spilled on the stove top, nearby,
reading, you, you whose thighs I love.
This mist descended in darkness
and the houselights stare like
watery eyes that seep streams
over the cool surface so stagnant
I imagine the lives here
in heavy sills of soaked wood.
Mapping patterns in sidewalk tremors
rising with the root of a sugar maple
the shadows give to bricks, the moon
is back, it's irrepressible! There go
the stragglers home to some episodes
and there go the runners, ball to toe
as they go, past the students, leaf gatherers
and the popular unambitious drunks.

White Death This Exit

I.

Silver light posts arc over the road, white glare
beside a swift congruous river of red lights.
The moon is muffled but full. In storm,
or close to it, everyone going somewhere still.

Northbound highway is promotion and egress:
tree lines, hip roofs, glow of holiday lights
strung on houses, strung upon shrubs, candles
burn or electric candles "on" behind windows,

votives and voices, dashboard speakers.
Rational voices from national radio.
A view of office towers, advertising, the
roads that lead to steel and glass plazas.

A close storm, around Xmas, everything
will close when it strikes. Seventy
per cent of tomahawk tip oxidized
and aerated. A sort of exit. A wooden

shaft 2 ½ feet long, stone tip
sharpened at one end. Air raided.
Sortie. Mufflers wrapped of an evening.
Poison belch into "crisp" air.

Two planes of chimney meet: west side
snow-covered, the north side only wet.

To blow tomahawks: to kill or cut.
He "sunk his hatchet into his brains"

tho the victim was his kin. A terrible night
the sky and the noise seeming like the cries,
the glare of flintlock by firelight. Trigger.
As thunder. Surgically bombed.

Latin, from stem of *mittere*, to send.
Patriot, from Andover: "war means jobs."
Snowfall covers the jagged, busted glass.
Savage, cling, clung or stick

lintel amid brick piling
obsequious in lit corners, rub
panes scratched with a wet branch,
frozen-bristled, rigid in wind.

The natives nationalized livestock and corn.
Clams free for the raking. Slush streets a sleek
frozen surface, a sluice on Sunday, next day
the papers repeat: *tougher on Iraq,* tiny

frozen drift, spittle, white ragged drop, like ash.
Vaporization and dust. A black star shot
and smeared, the man's ground body,
only the head remained, eyes shut looking up.

Endicott in Connecticut
waged a brilliant terror campaign
destroying crops of Pequots.
Bush's band of grim men.

2.

Light refractory highway
moon muffled by cloud gap
hurtle its mist, blackness
of valley held under the surface,

blue twilight obscured
against the shade of those hills.
Thru it a seamless snaking of road,
brilliantly lit, surging or greased

in docility, treatment, a capable
reckoning violence, its sandstone
canvas uniform, photographs in wallet.
What makes a land promised?

Predestined spasms of nation
in their rhetoric, in their ears;
indelible units of folk
pre-packaged creed and wrap,

meta-tyranny, weaponry steep
flails with purpose against non-peoples,
strategizes consent, shoveled deep,
crumbling piles; resembles to a child

a reasonable iceberg to place
some plastic figurines
of classical cowboys and Indians;
contemporary Arabs and Marines.

A leader elected, steeped in oil, its politics,
education, a polity, wanting severe, civility,
the education president, schooled at Yale,
he said of King Philip "we cannot

reward an aggressor" and gathered allies,
potential allies, Xtian converts at Natick,
praying Arabs. This is Increase Mather
speaking: "it will not stand."

Able to kill several hundred Pequots
with only a handful of losses to
themselves. "With one blow of his
hatchet dispatched him."

3.

Victory: highly respirable;
dermal, oral, pulmonary portal.
In wounds, burns, retained in lungs,
ingested, absorbed in blood.

No one ever calls the president "asshole"
on television, on radio, in newspapers;
nor murderer, expediter, pieface,
nor bootlick, saver-of-face, executor

of that which is opportune; in terms
of scandal or flattery, enjoining the nation,
rejoining it "to heal." Why don't they
say what it is like to be bombed

by the United States for ten years?
Let it be said with the persistence
of a semen-stained dress. Ten years
without potable water, an infrastructure

destroyed, its reconstruction blocked
until you rise to kill
          your own brutal dictator?
If you agree to murder
          your own cruel ruler,
why stop there? And not quash

the pre-fab "democracy" in packing crates
awaiting installation? Jet engine scream
on tarmac. Stuck in nimbus of brick,
blew in the fired walls: today,

a view from the bridge, palisades
collapsing as they flee from the fort.
Savage, merciless, tomahawk.
This is Peter Arnett, bleeding from the head,

in the Great Cedar Swamp of Rhode Island.
The musket balls will burn for a billion years.
Just a whiff of tobacco before it ends
and they sunk a hatchet into his brains.

Shot face down in wetlands, sold
overseas, with crumpled bill of sale
in hand: sarin, soman, anthrax. Waving
flag and gun for god and justice.

4.

Gone the white fat flakes that fell
scraped apogee in afternoon's saturate
gray; fine and few the snowfall now,
the airlines failed to cease. Light

increase, surge and falter, flicker,
a filter to pitch. Winter evening of
New Hampshire. On ground the grain
in the water, the bits, and from the sky,

primitive in ideology, flint for flaking
fire, the flack, residual facts
esophagus tissue lined with sand.
Watch now. Something stirs.

Satellites reel graceful ellipsis.
Baby incubators Wampanoags
unplugged you can see them
from the frontier of your yard

or fence the world is so small,
able to launch or lob like a hand toy
a parcel bearing a rupturous gift.
Scorched ruins to witness from your frontier.

A swamp that is long, wide not so deep
a horde cannot traverse it, carrying
trappings on their backs beside giant trees
that have died here, remain, bare boughs

hold a heaviness of osprey nests in thick clusters.
Just as Mistress Rowlandson is about to quit
for fatigue Metacomet slips up and
offers his hand. She does not refuse.

So the Wampanoags learned death, a private property.
Ferocity in warfare, in kind, outwash Pleistocene till
crumbling since the "Indian Wars" behind a Mobil.
Non-fissionable nuclear attacks clear disasters for centuries.

Walk patches half melt. For civilians,
veterans: four and a half-billion-
year half-life. Promised peace for surrender
but sold as slaves out of country.

Marketing appeal, everyone calls upon God.
Vietnam Syndrome negated, Gulf War
Syndrome created. One symptom of one
syndrome is conscience; the other syndrome

attacks the nervous system. Clouds troop
over office towers. Leaves fallen forcefully
in storm. It must be quite a storm. Sinister
light in blue bursts. A powerful thrust.

[2000-2001]

Daniel Bouchard lives in Somerville, Massachusetts. His first book, *Diminutive Revolutions* (2000), is available from Subpress.